# *Resurrection: The Good Pursuits*

***A JOURNEY TO REACH NIRVANA WITH JOYCE POAG***

# Contents

# Preface

*[22] Then Jesus said to his disciples: "Therefore I tell you, do not worry about your life, what you will eat; or about your body, what you will wear.*

*[23] For life is more than food, and the body more than clothes.*

*[24] Consider the ravens: They do not sow or reap, they have no storeroom or barn; yet God feeds them. And how much more valuable you are than birds!*

*[25] Who of you by worrying can add a single hour to your life?*

*[26] Since you cannot do this very little thing, why do you worry about the rest?*

[27] *Consider how the wild flowers grow. They do not labor or spin. Yet I tell you, not even Solomon in all his splendor was dressed like one of these.*

*— Luke 12:22-27*

Is the glass half empty or half full? I know that's a cliché, but it is the best litmus test to define one's attitude. I am a "glass half full" type of person, and I never like to spend or rather waste my time, my life, my thoughts on negative things. Life is a precious gift of God, and it is not long enough to be wasted on negative emotions. There are lots of good things to do, so why waste it on negative thoughts.

When we look around ourselves, we can find too many things that can bother us and invoke negative feelings, that can force us to be frustrated, agitated, and lose hope for betterment.  And this is when the "glass half empty" attitude overcomes us. We are too worried about our worldly desires and keep on working hard to achieve success according to our own parameters. In reality, the real success lies in fulfilling God's commands and follow His ways instead of our created ways.

Today, worldly success does matter to us but should it really matter to us?

Is the purpose of our life on this earth to achieve good things for ourselves?

Do we really know what our mission is on this earth?

There are so many questions in our lives, and we roam frantically here and there to find their true answers. But every answer is hidden in plain sight, and we need to open our inner eye to see and understand them.

When I meet people, I often hear them complaining about the hardships of life, and they are going through lots of pressure to survive emotionally, physically, and financially. Yes, there are hardships, and life is never going to be a bed of roses, and it never was for Jesus Christ, literally. We can never be pious enough to match our spirituality and goodness to that of Jesus Christ, so how can we even think of a trouble-free life. Yet there are millions of people who are lucky enough to spend a life with almost no troubles. As I quoted a verse *(Luke 12:22-27)* above, God is here to take care of this universe and everything in it. He is never negligent of His duties and has a plan for every person, and His plans are the best plans.

There is no harm in pursuing our dreams, and I encourage you to do so. I had this dream of joining the medicine industry, and I am a professional in medicine today. I had my difficulties on the way and faced them with the help of God as He gave me enough courage and strength to pursue my dream. Thus, we need to pursue our dreams by following the ways God has told us. He is the best guide for us in this whole world, and He will never abandon us, come what may! At times, our pursuits trap us and make us focus on ourselves, and we are left with nothing at the end. We have this life to share with others and let them be a good part of our lives, and that's what God wants us to do.

> [35] *For I was hungry and you gave me something to eat, I was thirsty and you gave me something to drink, I was a stranger and you invited me in,*

*[36] I needed clothes and you clothed me, I was sick and you looked after me, I was in prison and you came to visit me.' [37] "Then the righteous will answer him, 'Lord, when did we see you hungry and feed you, or thirsty and give you something to drink? [38] When did we see you a stranger and invite you in, or needing clothes and clothe you? [39] When did we see you sick or in prison and go to visit you?' [40] "The King will reply, 'Truly I tell you, whatever you did for one of the least of these brothers and sisters of mine, you did for me.'*

*— Matthew 25:35-40*

Thus, we actually get closer to God when we help others and bring comfort to others. In fact, when we do so, we benefit ourselves, and our good deeds cause a universal effect to yield goodness. This circle of goodness can get bigger and bigger if we play our part with a pure heart and soul.

God has given us hope, the best tool to drive away every evil force, and fulfill our lives with a healthy and positive attitude. God is our strength and a true savior for us, and it is WE who have been turning a blind eye to His commandments. The moment we follow our Lord, we are relieved of our fears, anxiety, anger, and every bad emotion we may have, and we are filled with happiness, success, affection, and positivity.

I see people talking about how bad they are, and they will not be forgiven. If you also believe so, let me tell you that it is a baseless concept. Our Lord, our Savior is merciful and forgiving, and He never abandons us; Instead, He waits for us to repent so that

He can bestow us with forgiveness. Jesus Christ gave His life for our sins, so how can we, His followers, be left alone in agony?

> *Teaching them to observe all that I have commanded you. And behold, I am with you always, to the end of the age."*
>
> *— Matthew 28:20*

Hence, He is always there for us, so how can we abandon such a merciful Lord?

There are plenty of encouraging promises, which we will explore in this book, that God has made to us and He always keeps his word. Let's start this journey to reach nirvana and real success in life with a pure heart and soul together, Amen.

# Chapter 1: The Web of Worldly Pursuits

> *[15] Do not love the world or anything in the world. If anyone loves the world, love for the Father is not in them.*
>
> *[16] For everything in the world — the lust of the flesh, the lust of the eyes, and the pride of life — comes not from the Father but from the world.*
>
> *[17] The world and its desires pass away, but whoever does the will of God lives forever.*
>
> *— 1 John 2:15-17*

God has bestowed us with this great and beautiful world and life, and He has not forbidden us to relish the worldly joys at all. If they weren't for us, why would He create these great things around us?

The problems do not lie with the worldly things and the desire to get them, but these problems originate when we make them our primary objective; when we forget our Lord who is the actual master and provider of these things; when we blur the line between right and wrong; and when we violate others' rights to achieve our objectives.

This web of worldly pursuits, such as money, fame, and lust, has been a part of human beings since the beginning of humanity, and it seems to grow over time. Today, we are hopelessly trapped in this web of pursuits just to be happy while the happiness does not seem to be on speaking terms with us. Because money and fame without the love of God cannot get us anywhere but to a downward spiral.

*The seed that fell among thorns stands for those who hear, but as they go on their way they are choked by life's worries, riches and pleasures, and they do not mature.*

*— Luke 8:14*

When I talk to people and read different kinds of literature, they all talk about how advanced our world has become. Today, we can do things about which our ancestors did not even have the slightest idea. Technologically speaking, yes, we are at the greatest heights of advancements. We have the fastest means of communication and travel, and we have reduced labor work with the help of high-tech machines. We have landed on the moon, and we are aiming to find life on Mars. It all sounds great, and it is! Everything is great, right?

Today, there are more progressive opportunities for jobs and businesses. Many economies are booming, and the countries are developing. Compared to the past, everything is ahead, and it is actually good. Have advancement and technology removed our issues, i.e., war, violence, and famine in various parts of our world, anxiety, stress, and many other problems? Are we happy with what we have achieved? At what cost, have we achieved it all? There are so many questions that we need to answer if we really want to have content, happy lives where we are rich spiritually.

> *Do not conform to the pattern of this world, but be transformed by the renewing of your mind. Then you will be able to test and approve what*

*God's will is—his good, pleasing and perfect will.*

*— Romans 12:2*

Using smart devices is a common sight today. Do the devices we use every day spare us enough time to even listen to God's words? The answer is disappointing. In fact, we listen to our devices and love them more than our Creator. In no way, I am asking you to become a hermit and abandon this world. I never meant it. We are here to obey and serve God, and we have to do it in the world around us that always tempts us to leave the good path.

Even Adam and Eve fell victims to the worldly joys in the Garden of Eden, and Cain killed Abel out of jealousy when his sacrifice was not accepted by God. The serpent cunningly convinced Eve to eat the fruit from the forbidden tree, and she did eat the fruit and also offered Adam to eat. Thus, they lost the pleasure of living in Eden.

> *When the woman saw that the fruit of the tree was good for food and pleasing to the eye, and also desirable for gaining wisdom, she took some and ate it. She also gave some to her husband, who was with her, and he ate it.*
>
> *— Genesis 3:6*
>
> *After Adam and Eve had disobeyed God, "the eyes of both of them were opened, and they realized they were naked; so they sewed fig leaves together and made coverings for themselves.*
>
> *— Genesis 3:7*

*It wasn't long after that they hid from God, as it says, "Then the man and his wife heard the sound of the Lord God as he was walking in the garden in the cool of the day, and they hid from the Lord God among the trees of the garden.*
*— Genesis 3:8*

*To the woman he said, "I will make your pains in childbearing very severe with painful labor you will give birth to children. Your desire will be for your husband, and he will rule over you.*
*— Genesis 3:16*

*[17] To Adam he said, "Because you listened to your wife and ate fruit from the tree about which I commanded you, 'You must not eat from it,' Cursed is the ground because of you;*

*through painful toil you will eat food from it all the days of your life. [18] It will produce thorns and thistles for you, and you will eat the plants of the field. [19] By the sweat of your brow you will eat your food until you return to the ground, since from it you were taken; for dust you are and to dust you will return."*

*— Genesis 3:17-19*

The first couple on this universe pursued their desire, and they got severe punishments. Look at us now! We are overfilled with our wants and desires, and many of us blur the difference between right and wrong in this rat race. Adam and Eve were the great ones, but they, too, made a mistake. They immediately realized, they repented, and they were forgiven. No matter how big or small a sin you have committed to pursue your desires, or you have just forgotten to spare time to pray to God or follow His commands, God is always here waiting to forgive you, and give you another chance to start obeying His commands. I can assure you that once you are on God's way, you will become the most content and happiest person on the face of the earth. Remember that this world is an ephemeral place for us.

> *But the day of the Lord will come like a thief, and then the heavens will pass away with a roar, and the heavenly bodies will be burned up and dissolved, and the earth and the works that are done on it will be exposed. Since all these things are thus to be dissolved, what sort of people ought you to be in lives of holiness and godliness, waiting for and hastening the coming*

*of the day of God, because of which the heavens will be set on fire and dissolved, and the heavenly bodies will melt as they burn! But according to his promise we are waiting for new heavens and a new earth in which righteousness dwells.*

*— 2 Peter 3:10-13*

# Chapter 2: Hope: Our First Line of Defense

*[35] As Jesus approached Jericho, a blind man was sitting by the roadside begging. 36 When he heard the crowd going by, he asked what was happening.*

*[37] They told him, "Jesus of Nazareth is passing by."*

*[38] He called out, "Jesus, Son of David, have mercy on me!"*

*[39] Those who led the way rebuked him and told him to be quiet, but he shouted all the more, "Son of David, have mercy on me!"*

*[40] Jesus stopped and ordered the man to be brought to him. When he came near, Jesus asked him, [41] "What do you want me to do for you?" "Lord, I want to see," he replied.*

*[42] Jesus said to him, "Receive your sight; your faith has healed you."*
*[43] Immediately he received his sight and followed Jesus, praising God. When all the people saw it, they also praised God.*
*— Luke 18:35-43*

When I read this verse, it consolidates my faith in hope, and I wish I could hope just like this blind man. I consider this verse as a classic example of hope. This verse teaches us a simple lesson of believing in God and Jesus Christ. We simply need to call Jesus for help with hope, and we will be answered positively. When you run low of hope, turn to the bible, and you will have a refreshing way of hoping for the best. He was a blind man, so he never saw Jesus, but he believed in the hope and truth that Jesus brought to us.

In an instant, he was rewarded for his call. This is how we need to have faith in hope.

At times, life becomes too difficult, and it is hard to hold on to hope. Again, that is our pursuit for worldly joys that hinder our way, and we believe that hope is lost, and we turn to pessimism or aggression. When we lose hope, we actually deviate from the way of God and make a mistake and sin. But the bible verses are the eternal sources of hope that keep us encouraged and remind us of how hope can work for us. We hope that after we have lived this life for Jesus, we will be with Him everlastingly, and this is what we live for. And this is a reality that demands us to focus on things set in the heavenly places instead of the worldly things.

*And the God of all grace, who called you to his eternal glory in Christ, after you have suffered a little while, will himself restore you and make you strong, firm and steadfast.*

*— 1 Peter 5:10*

*Whoever sows to please their flesh, from the flesh will reap destruction; whoever sows to please the Spirit, from the Spirit will reap eternal life.*

*— Galatians 6:8*

We are the creation of God, so He is well aware of our vulnerabilities, and we toil to find and hold onto hope, especially in the times of crisis. When we face a test of faith, the strongest ones find it difficult to see and hold onto hope. As a human being, we are weak, and we need to be reminded from time to time of the hope that God offers us in the bible. This way, we can live a life that God wants us to live.

> *If then you were raised with Christ, seek those things which are above, where Christ is, sitting at the right hand of God. Set your mind on things above, not on things on the earth.*
>
> *— Colossians 3:1-2*

In various dictionaries, when we look up the meaning of hope, we find the definition as:

- A feeling of expectation and desire for a particular thing to happen
- Something good that you want to happen in the future
- A confident feeling about what will happen in the future

In our simple languages, hope is a feeling of expecting something to happen, but the speaker is never 100% certain about that thing to happen. It could be 99%, but never 100%. When we talk about biblical hope, it is not about a feeling that lacks certainty. The biblical hope is a 100% guarantee of that happening. The biblical hope does not come from a common person like us, but it is from the Creator of the universe. When God speaks to Jesus Christ and to us, there is no uncertainty in His words. God's words are definite, and they happen when He wills. When God asks to have hope, He actually promises us to deliver it because He does not need permission from others, but others need His permission. It is quite easy for us to lose hope in our world that is full of sins and sufferings, but we need to have hope in the biblical sense, and we will get whatever we hope for.

*[1] Therefore, since we have been justified through faith, we have peace with God through our Lord Jesus Christ,*

*[2] through whom we have gained access by faith into this grace in which we now stand. And we boast in the hope of the glory of God.*

*[3] Not only so, but we also glory in our sufferings, because we know that suffering produces perseverance;*

*[4] perseverance, character; and character, hope.*

*[5] And hope does not put us to shame, because God's love has been poured out into our hearts through the Holy Spirit, who has been given to us.*

*— Romans 5:1-5*

Thus, I say that hope is our first defense against despair and sufferings. With hope, we can see the miracles happening around us. In modern times, we find no example of women bearing at the age of 90 or even 80. The oldest woman to give birth is 72 from India in 2016. But Sarah gave birth at the age of 90 years. It happened because God made Abraham a promise that Sarah would be a mother of nations.

> *I will bless her and will surely give you a son by her. I will bless her so that she will be the mother of nations; kings of peoples will come from her.*
>
> *— Genesis 17:16*

Sarah, the wife of Abraham and mother of Isaac, was childless until the age of 90. Both believed that they would never become parents. But God had a greater plan for them, so God promised Abraham that Sarah would conceive and bear a son. Thus, Isaac was born in their old age. Sarah and Abraham believed in God's words, because they had faith and hope in God's words.

*And by faith even Sarah, who was past childbearing age, was enabled to bear children because she considered him faithful who had made the promise.*

*— Hebrews 11:11*

Jesus and prophets never doubted the words of God, and they never lost hope, no matter how difficult the circumstances were. Today, we can read the bible, which tells lots of miraculous happenings, such as the one told at the beginning of this chapter of Jericho, the blind man. With hope, we can always have enough strength to fix every bad thing in our lives.

> *Do not be afraid—I am with you! I am your God—let nothing terrify you! I will make you strong and help you; I will protect you and save you.*
>
> *— Isaiah 41:10*

## Chapter 3: Anxiety

*[19] "Do not store up for yourselves treasures on earth, where moths and vermin destroy, and where thieves break in and steal.*

*[20] But store up for yourselves treasures in heaven, where moths and vermin do not destroy, and where thieves do not break in and steal.*

*[21] For where your treasure is, there your heart will be also.*

*— Matthew 6:19-21*

Today, we are quite familiar with words like stress, pressure, and anxiety. A few decades back, these words, in fact, diseases seemed to be nonexistent, at least they were not common like they are today.

We may not realize, but chronic worry can really cause health issues like ulcers, heart attack, and high blood pressure. According to Dr. Charles Mayo, worry can affect the circulation, the heart, the glands, and the whole nervous system. He further says that one may not die of overtask, but one can die of worry. So, we can worry ourselves to death. Anxiety is the most common psychological problem in the USA. It affects 40 million grownups in the USA. Though anxiety is treatable, only 36.9% receive treatment for anxiety.

> *I have told you these things, so that in Me you may have peace. In this world you will have trouble. But take heart! I have overcome the world.*

*— John 16:33*

Anxiety is distress about forthcoming reservations. It is characterized by psychological nervousness and restlessness. Largely, it concerns people with the thought of what might happen in the future. It is mainly caused by threats and fears to our wellbeing, whether real or unreal, as we feel vulnerable against these threats and fears. These threats and fears include social rejection, physical injuries, poverty, and death, among others. There are three main elements of anxiety, and they are Insecurity, Helplessness, and Isolation.

*There among those nations you will find no peace or place to rest. And the LORD will cause your heart to tremble, your eyesight to fail, and your soul to despair.*

*— Deuteronomy 28:65*

Anxiety directly indicates that you doubt God's power and mercy for you. It makes us helpless and keeps you troubled. The solution lies in the bible and believing in God and Jesus. We feel scared all the time, and it is a central element of anxiety.

*Your life will constantly hang in the balance. You will live night and day in fear, unsure if you will survive.*

*— Deuteronomy 28:66*

To overcome anxiety, the best is to trust in God!

If you treat the symptoms, the issue will resurface soon enough; thus, we need to focus on finding the root causes to get rid of anxiety for good. You will find many people who will give you solutions, such as go on vacation, switch to a less demanding job, and the like. But anxiety is inside you, so wherever you go, you are accompanying it with yourself. Hence, the solution must come from inside, and then the other solutions will work too.

To overcome anxiety, firstly, trust in God, and this is the best plan for your redemption and deliverance.

When you trust God, you are secure, you have the most powerful entity for help, and you will never be alone when you have God on your side.

*[5] Keep your lives free from the love of money and be content with what you have, because God has said, "Never will I leave you; never will I forsake you. [6] The Lord is my helper; I will not be afraid. What can mere mortals do to me?*

*— Hebrews 13:5-6*

*God is the one who has power over all, and we must have absolute faith and confidence in God's powers if we want to deal with every issue in our life.*

*I can do everything through him who gives me strength.*

*— Philippians 4:13*

The best step to start treating anxiety comes through prayer, and it is an open option for all. Prayer is a direct request to ask God for help. You need to have confidence that when you approach God for help for anything, He will hear you. It is another promise of God that He will send peace of mind to every person who is eager to seek help from God to end their anxieties.

> [6] *Do not be anxious about anything, but in every situation, by prayer and petition, with thanksgiving, present your requests to God.* [7] *And the peace of God, which transcends all understanding, will guard your hearts and your minds in Christ Jesus.*
>
> *— Philippians 4:6-7*

We need to realize that everything in this world and the things you possess and your relations are impermanent. One day, they will be lost, broken, burned, etc. The only, the most important, and the permanent thing in life is our relationship with God. If you treasure this relationship, there will be nothing to worry about in your life. Whatever you do for God, it is stored in Heaven and will be a source of salvation for you at the end. Our God is our master, and we are the servant who must obey.

> *No one can serve two masters. Either you will hate the one and love the other, or you will be devoted to the one and despise the other. You cannot serve both God and money.*
>
> — *Matthew 6:24*

# Chapter 4: Fears, Justified?

*He will never leave you nor forsake you. Do not be afraid; do not be discouraged."*

*— Deuteronomy 31:8*

Fear is a feeling that hinders us from doing and accomplishing many things in life. Fear discourages us to even perform an activity, and we accept defeat without participating. Fear is a genuine feeling, and there is nothing to be ashamed of it, and there is nothing to hide as well. The problems arise when we try to hide our fears, and we fall short of whatever we do.

Today, we are surrounded by many fears such as fear of losing friends and family, falling sick, low living standard, death, financial loss, among others.

There is a long list of fears whose mere thought paralyze us. However, we often miss the fear that we must have, the fear of our God. In the bible, the fear of God is considered the start of wisdom.

> *Do not be afraid of those who kill the body but cannot kill the soul. Rather, be afraid of the One who can destroy both soul and body in hell.*
>
> *— Matthew 10:28*

We are worried about the wrath of our bosses when we make a mistake or do not perform well at work. We are afraid of making our friends and family members angry and take extreme care to avoid such situations. But this intensity of fear is absent when it comes to obeying God while we know that He does not like us to go astray and indulge in sin. In spite of knowing it all, we ignore His commands and continue our life doing the wrong things. We must have holy fear because he is the only Judge of our actions and has the power to determine our fates. But deep in our hearts, we know how gracious and merciful He is, and we take advantage of His mercy.

Fear is a negative feeling and weakens a person, but this is not the case with the fear of God. In fact, it is the form of fear that gives us the strength to do the right things, always. All kinds of ungodly fears ruin us mentally, physically, socially, and spiritually. If you have a fear of sickness, it will beget more mental and physical health issues, and I can tell you that anxiety is one of the worst issues. When you have a fear of death, it will make your life dull. You will not be able to see the sources of joy and happiness.

God tells us not to be afraid of the ungodly sources of fears, and the people who fear do not understand this. We have many feelings in our heart, and fear is one of them. There are some things that cannot exist at the same time. If there is light, there is no darkness and vice versa. You can understand that fear is darkness, and love is light. The Bible further explains how it is possible to remove our fears.

> *There is no fear in love; but perfect love casts out fear, because fear involves torment. But he who fears has not been made perfect in love.*
> *— 1 John 4:18*

Every person has some sort of fear in his heart, and there is a huge variety of fears. To get rid of our fears, we need to realize the basic problems that trigger those fears. The issue with our fears is not actually the fear, but what they show about our concept of God. If we have fears of any kind, we, in fact, have no trust in God. Our fears indicate that we doubt God's power and promises and what He has planned for us. We fail miserably to identify that He is the only One worthy of being feared because He is above all. He deserves to be revered, trusted, and loved. Ask for forgiveness if you have a fear of ungodly sources and of not having trust in Him. When you fear God, there will be nothing else in this world that can frighten you.

> *Don't fear, for I have redeemed you; I have called you by name; you are Mine.*
>
> *—Isaiah 43:1*

Just like dark vanishes when there is light, fear vanishes when we fill our heart with the love of God.

When Abraham feared his enemies, God consoled him:

> *Do not be afraid, Abram. I am your shield, your very great reward*
>
> *— Genesis 15:1*

When Hagar feared famine, God said to her,

> *[17] God heard the boy crying, and the angel of God called to Hagar from heaven and said to her, "What is the matter, Hagar? Do not be afraid; God has heard the boy crying as he lies there. [18] Lift the boy up and take him by the hand, for I will make him into a great*

*nation.” [19] Then God opened her eyes and she saw a well of water. So she went and filled the skin with water and gave the boy a drink.*

*— Genesis 21:17-19*

When Jacob was in disbelief:

*I am God, the God of your father,” he said. “Do not be afraid to go down to Egypt, for I will make you into a great nation there. 4 I will go down to Egypt with you, and I will surely bring you back again. And Joseph’s own hand will close your eyes.*

*— Genesis 46:3-4*

When Moses faced the Red Sea:

> *Moses answered the people, "Do not be afraid. Stand firm and you will see the deliverance the Lord will bring you today. The Egyptians you see today you will never see again.*
>
> *— Exodus 14:13*

Jesus always spoke each and every word with a purpose, and He repeated his words on purpose to lay emphasis on his teachings. One thing that he often repeated is about no fear. On many occasions, he said phrases such as "Fear not," "Be not afraid," and "Do not be anxious."

Jesus is a positive energy, a light that luminates our paths and lives. So, Jesus always helps us remove the darkness that is growing inside our minds and souls and in our surroundings. Thus, Jesus tells us repeatedly to follow his path, and we will not need to fear an evil and negative force or people.

# Chapter 5: Forgive Others, Move On

*[3] So watch yourselves. "If your brother or sister sins against you, rebuke them; and if they repent, forgive them.*

*[4] Even if they sin against you seven times in a day and seven times come back to you saying 'I repent,' you must forgive them."*

*— Luke 17:3-4*

When we recite the Lord's Prayer, we read a line that makes us think about forgiving others.

*Forgive us our sins as we also forgive those who sin against us.*

As we finish the Lord's Prayer, we find the following words in Matthew 6:14-15.

> *For if you forgive men when they sin against you, your heavenly Father will also forgive you. But if you do not forgive men their sins, your Father will not forgive your sins.*

These are very important verses about understanding the importance of forgiving others and moving on. These verses reveal the yardstick that God uses to forgive us. Forgiving others is a tough call. At times, people do things to others that hurt badly, and it is never easy to forget about those bad things, but forgiving is for our own good. I think that we have a hard time when it comes to forgiving others since we do not really understand what it means to forgive others. To get a clear picture, we can first see what forgiving others is not.

Firstly, when you forgive others, you do not justify their actions. If you have been hurt by others, you may not need to say what they did was alright because they could have been under stress because of some other reason and you just happened to be the victim to their anger. This way, you do not justify their anger, and they realize what they did was wrong.

Secondly, it is not about the idea that things will get better as time passes. Time does fade the memory of the incidence, but it may not heal the wound. You may have an opposing viewpoint, but I think that passing time only is not enough.

Thirdly, when somebody hurts you, it is painful, and the memory lasts for a good number of days or even years. Thus, when you forgive others, it may not mean you deny being hurt. Whether you are a man or woman, bad things hurt both, though men tend to deny that they are hurt and they say that they do not care. So, do not say that they did not hurt you. They certainly did, and this is why you forgive those people.

Fourthly, when you forgive others, it is not about opposing and trying to extract a response, especially an apology. When you forgive, the apology will come itself. Thus, you do not twist their arm and ask for an apology. You are not avenging on somebody and trying to cause emotional or physical harm. Forgiveness is above past revenge and harm.

Now let's talk about what it really means to forgive others! It starts with the realization of how you have been forgiven in the past and how God has forgiven you so far. I can say that we may not be able to count the times God has forgiven us. The best part about God's forgiveness is that it comes in a complete form.

God's forgiveness is unconditional because He does not need us, but we do. The only condition He applies is that you forgive others. And when you want to forgive others, ensure that you have been forgiven as well. Since the bible is our guide to understand life and everything in it, Jesus has a great parable to tells us about how forgiveness works. It is called the Parable of the Unmerciful Servant.

> *[21] Then Peter came to Jesus and asked, "Lord, how many times shall I forgive my brother or sister who sins against me? Up to seven times?"*
>
> *[22] Jesus answered, "I tell you, not seven times, but seventy-seven times.*
>
> *[23] "Therefore, the kingdom of heaven is like a king who wanted to settle accounts with his servants. [24] As he began the settlement, a man who owed him ten*

*thousand bags of gold was brought to him.* [25] *Since he was not able to pay, the master ordered that he and his wife and his children and all that he had be sold to repay the debt.*

[26] *"At this the servant fell on his knees before him. 'Be patient with me,' he begged, 'and I will pay back everything.'* [27] *The servant's master took pity on him, canceled the debt and let him go.*

[28] *"But when that servant went out, he found one of his fellow servants who owed him a hundred silver coins. He grabbed him and began to choke him. 'Pay back what you owe me!' he demanded.*

*[29] "His fellow servant fell to his knees and begged him, 'Be patient with me, and I will pay it back.'*

*[30] "But he refused. Instead, he went off and had the man thrown into prison until he could pay the debt. [31] When the other servants saw what had happened, they were outraged and went and told their master everything that had happened.*

*[32] "Then the master called the servant in. 'You wicked servant,' he said, 'I canceled all that debt of yours because you begged me to. [33] Shouldn't you have had mercy on your fellow servant just as I had on you?' [34] In anger his master handed him over to the jailers to be*

*tortured, until he should pay back all he owed.*

[35] *"This is how my heavenly Father will treat each of you unless you forgive your brother or sister from your heart.*

*— Matthew 18:21-35*

I need you to read the last verse (Matthew 18: 35) again, and preferably, a few more times and focus on its words and meanings. When you pay attention closely, you will find that it is a serious admonition for us. The last verse in this parable emphasizes on forgiving others, or else we will not be forgiven. Thus, when you forgive others, you actually forgive yourself.

If you have any person in mind who did something bad to you, and you should forgive him or her, take a generous step now and forgive them all. Forget the bad memories, throw away the grudge, and embrace them. I see forgiveness as a boomerang. When you throw it, it comes right back to you. So, it is an absolute win-win situation for everyone involved.

Again, I would say that it will not be an easy task to do, but it is worthwhile. You have already endured physical or mental pain and abuse, humiliation, infidelity, or betrayal, but that time is gone. You cannot harbor a grudge or ill feelings in your heart for others. If you do so, they will keep rotting you inside.

When you are ready to forgive others who caused you pain, think of how you have been forgiven by God and by other people. Your forgiveness is complete when you release others. It means that you let them go and move on. You stop harping on your pain and blaming the other person. Bury that unfortunate incident forever! Burn that painful tape in your mind! This is how you release others. If you say that you have forgiven, but you hold a grudge against them, that's not forgiveness! God does not forgive you this way. Grudge is a cancerous disease, and it grows over time and possesses your mind, body, and soul. Let it go and cleanse your heart of the grudge and ill feelings about others. Thus, forgive others and release them fully.

> *You shall not take vengeance or bear a grudge against the sons of your own people, but you shall love your neighbor as yourself: I am the Lord.*
>
> *— Leviticus 19:18*

Forgiveness is a wise choice because it also brings you freedom. It is tough, but there are some psychological ways to do it with ease. For instance, take a paper, sit down, write a letter to the one who has hurt you. Write whatever you want to say to that person and wanted to say at that time. Leave out no feelings. End this letter by writing that you release that person. Now put the letter in an envelope and, instead of mailing it, put it in File 13 mailbox. It may sound a weird or stupid act, but it works. It can also be a rehearsal to actually forgive the one in person.

In another way, you can imagine having a dialogue with that person and end the meeting by saying that "I forgive you, and I release you." My point is that you take every step, anything that can help you forgive and release others because this is what God wants us to do.

> [17] *Do not repay anyone evil for evil. Be careful to do what is right in the eyes of everyone.* [18] *If it is possible, as far as it depends on you, live at peace with everyone.* [19] *Do not take revenge, my dear friends, but leave room for God's wrath, for it is written: "It is mine to avenge; I will repay," says the Lord.* [20] *On the contrary, if your enemy is*

*hungry, feed him; if he is thirsty, give him something to drink. In doing this, you will heap burning coals on his head.* [21] *Do not be overcome by evil, but overcome evil with good.*

*— Romans 12:17-21*

Here you can see that revenge is not our job because God has taken this job as He says in Romans 12:19. When God has declared His promise, why bother and smolder from pain inside? Just say that the particular person owes me nothing now as I release him or her just like the king in the parable. If those people keep on doing bad things to others and do not forgive others, God's mills are grinding, and those people will have consequences.

Can you see that there is a greater role of God when we forgive others? Yes, God is with us when we forgive our wrongdoers and enemies. God is a great helper in this process. We get true freedom as we realize that we cannot forgive without God's help. As you decide to forgive others, you open the doors and get closer to God. This closeness sets you free from suffering that can last for your lifetime and move you toward a life of harmony and liberty.

Forgiveness is a lifelong practice because life will keep coming back to you with harms caused by others. I feel sorry to say that, but this is how life works for us because we are emotional beings, and we will feel hurt and neglected at times. But the bible is here to guide us for life. If you struggle in forgiving others, take help from the bible and Jesus, the true savior. Hence, we can say that forgiving others lets us stay with peace and freedom.

If you have forgiven all the people who have wronged you so far, there will be more in the future because we do not live in a perfect world. The word "perfect" suits to heavens. In this world, we can live a great life while a perfect life awaits us in the heavens.

> *Get rid of all bitterness, rage and anger, brawling and slander, along with every form of malice. Be kind and compassionate to one another, forgiving each other, just as in Christ God forgave you.*
>
> *— Ephesians 4:31-32*

# Chapter 6: Anger: The Evil That Causes More Evil Things

*[26] In your anger do not sin: Do not let the sun go down while you are still angry, [27] and do not give the devil a foothold.*

*[28] Anyone who has been stealing must steal no longer, but must work, doing something useful with their own hands, that they may have something to share with those in need.*

*[29] Do not let any unwholesome talk come out of your mouths, but only what is helpful for building others up according to their needs, that it may benefit those who listen.*

*[30] And do not grieve the Holy Spirit of God, with whom you were sealed for the day of redemption.*

*[31] Get rid of all bitterness, rage and anger, brawling and slander, along with every form of malice.*

*— Ephesians 4:26-31*

Anger is a serious issue in our society and can be a destructive thing in our life. When we are angry, we can damage ourselves and our own possessions because anger turns people literally blind to the possible consequences. Let me give you an example to understand it better.

A couple parked their car outside of their neighbor's house every day that blocked their gate. The neighboring woman got fed up with their constant, annoying practice. She repeatedly asked the couple to stop parking their car outside her gate. One day, she rose before dawn and found a new, black-colored car parked at the same spot. This sight blew her fuse, and she damaged the car very badly and slashed the tires out of anger. She returned to her bed with a smile on her face because she had got great revenge. Later that morning, her husband woke her up to show the present he got for her birthday, yes, a new, black-colored car which she had destroyed at dawn.

Yes, we may do unwise acts when we let our anger take hold of our mind. We do things that we wish we could reverse caused by anger. Every day, the majority of people struggle against losing control of themselves and falling victim to violent fits. During the day, there are many things that upset us such as not being able to start your vehicle in the morning, gossip about you doing rounds in your office, confrontation with family members, etc.

God is aware of our weaknesses and how we struggle in the area of controlling anger. God's words warn us of the dangers of anger. If you notice, you will see that "anger" is just one letter short of "danger."

> *Whoever is patient has great understanding, but one who is quick-tempered displays folly.*
> *— Proverbs 14:29*

> [21] *You have heard that it was said to those of old, 'You shall not murder; and whoever murders will be liable to judgment.'* [22] *But I say to you that everyone who is angry with his brother will be liable to judgment; whoever insults his brother will be liable to the council; and whoever says, 'You fool!' will be liable to the hell of fire.*

*— Matthew 5:21-22*

Here, Jesus tells us that the root cause of evil things is anger. It is evident that anger makes you do the wrong things. However, the feeling of anger is not a sin itself as it is hinted in Psalm 4:4:

*Be angry, and do not sin. Meditate within your heart on your bed, and be still.*

The above verse allows us to see the fact that anger does not mean that we sin, but you can be angry and still do not commit a sin. Thus, we can say that there is righteous anger and unrighteous anger. The anger becomes troublesome when it is for personal grudge and other negative feelings. Your anger falls in the category of righteousness if you are distressed over prevalent practices of sin and injustice. If you are angry at terrorists' attacks, child abuse, violence against men and women, street crimes, and so on.

God gets angry, and Jesus too got angry at certain occasions, and they are the perfect examples of righteous anger. In fact, God and Jesus teach us to be righteous, so we can never expect unrighteous anger from neither of them.

> *Before him there was no king like him who turned to the LORD with all his heart and with all his soul and with all his might, according to all the law of Moses; nor did any like him arise after him. However, the LORD did not turn from the fierceness of His great wrath with which His anger burned against Judah, because of all the provocations with which Manasseh had provoked Him. The LORD said, "I will*

*remove Judah also from My sight, as I have removed Israel And I will cast off Jerusalem, this city which I have chosen, and the temple of which I said, 'My name shall be there.'"*

*— 2 Kings 23:25-27*

*For the LORD'S indignation is against all the nations, And His wrath against all their armies; He has utterly destroyed them, He has given them over to slaughter.*

*— Isaiah 34:2*

When God is angry with a person or a nation, there can be no escape from His wrath. But God does not get angry until we cross the limits and show no sign of mending our ways. Many nations were destroyed because they exceeded their limits, constantly disobeyed God, and did not follow His commandments. Jesus also showed righteous anger once when he attended a synagogue service on the Sabbath.

> [1] *Another time Jesus went into the synagogue, and a man with a shriveled hand was there.*
> [2] *Some of them were looking for a reason to accuse Jesus, so they watched him closely to see if he would heal him on the Sabbath.* [3] *Jesus said to the man with the shriveled hand, "Stand up in front of everyone."*
> [4] *Then Jesus asked them, "Which is lawful on the Sabbath: to do good or to do evil, to save life or to kill?" But they remained silent.*
> [5] *He looked around at them in anger and, deeply distressed at their stubborn hearts, said*

*to the man, "Stretch out your hand." He stretched it out, and his hand was completely restored. [6] Then the Pharisees went out and began to plot with the Herodians how they might kill Jesus.*

*— Mark 3:1-6*

Jesus tells us to avoid unrighteous anger because it leads to sin and injustice, and these things make God angry. Anger is a feeling that should arise when we see sin and injustice. If it does not happen, we need to question our character because we are either with or against the unrighteous anger. So, Jesus prohibits anger that is produced with malicious intentions because it corrupts our hearts and minds, and it leaves no room for forgiveness. Such anger also yields grudge and bitterness in our hearts. It brings utter destruction, and it gets out of control. Unrighteous anger is harsh, hateful, and self-centered. We may speak harsh words and ill of others and even get physically violent in a fit of unrighteous anger. We can see a classic example of unrighteous anger in Genesis 4 where the story of Cain murdering Abel is told.

> *Now Abel kept flocks, and Cain worked the soil. [3] In the course of time Cain brought some of the fruits of the soil as an offering to the Lord. [4] And Abel also brought an offering—fat portions from some of the firstborn of his flock. The Lord looked with favor on Abel and his offering, [5] but on Cain and his offering he did not look with favor. So, Cain was very angry, and his face was downcast. [6] Then the Lord said*

*to Cain, "Why are you angry? Why is your face downcast? [7] If you do what is right, will you not be accepted? But if you do not do what is right, sin is crouching at your door; it desires to have you, but you must rule over it."*

*— Genesis 4:3-7*

If we experience unrighteous anger, there will be dire consequences. In Galatians 6:7, we have been told a straightforward rule of nature that "Do not be deceived: God cannot be mocked. A man reaps what he sows! Isn't it a simple rule to understand? Our actions breed reactions, and unrighteous anger is bound to cause troubles. There is another important point to consider, and it is about getting an even bigger impact on our anger. Anger always hurts people, and these people could be our friends, colleagues, and family members. Every act conducted in anger ends up in causing disasters.

Jesus always handled anger efficiently. People screamed at him and insulted him on various occasions, but Jesus Christ never reacted negatively, never struck back, and never even thought of taking such actions. Christ showed us practically how to handle anger. Jesus does live in our souls and minds, so we can learn to react like Jesus against anger. The only response he made was love and prayers for those people. When you are angry with anyone, leave it to God.

# Chapter 7: Sweep in Front of Your Own Door First

*[1] "Do not judge, or you too will be judged.*

*[2] For in the same way you judge others, you will be judged, and with the measure you use, it will be measured to you.*

*[3] "Why do you look at the speck of sawdust in your brother's eye and pay no attention to the plank in your own eye?*

*[4] How can you say to your brother, 'Let me take the speck out of your eye,' when all the time there is a plank in your own eye?*

*[5] You hypocrite, first take the plank out of your own eye, and then you will see clearly to remove the speck from your brother's eye.*

— *Matthew 7:1-5*

Today, we live in a world filled with people who are hasty when it comes to passing judgment on others while they do not bother to look at themselves first. The majority of us is quick to judge others based on their ethnicity, wealth, house, and past. We simply find it easy to judge others with a yardstick created by ourselves. If we honestly measure ourselves against God's yardstick, we will realize that we really are low in our deeds.

I regret to say that even the churches are not immune to criticism and judging. Even the church folk criticize each other and judge each other. How can we make a claim to know God and Jesus Christ? If we say that we know God, wear a suit on Sunday, visit a church, read a few holy verses and sing hymns, yet we may not claim that we are close to God.

The word judge means "to render a decision about someone or something based on either right or wrong info." Unfortunately, when we judge people in our surroundings, the information is false or wrong at most times.

Judging people is not our job, but it is the job most suitable for our God. He is our creator and knows us inside out. Judgment is a divine job, and God will bring the Judgment Day on us. It is His duty, so why intervene in it? Seriously, we need to account for ourselves to get rid of this bad habit and focus on building our own character.

> *[1] but Jesus went to the Mount of Olives. [2] At dawn he appeared again in the temple courts, where all the people gathered around him, and he sat down to teach them. [3] The*

*teachers of the law and the Pharisees brought in a woman caught in adultery. They made her stand before the group* [4] *and said to Jesus, "Teacher, this woman was caught in the act of adultery.* [5] *In the Law Moses commanded us to stone such women. Now what do you say?"*

[6] *They were using this question as a trap, in order to have a basis for accusing him.*

*But Jesus bent down and started to write on the ground with his finger.* [7] *When they kept on questioning him, he straightened up and said to them, "Let anyone of you who is without sin be the first to throw a stone at her."* [8] *Again he stooped down and wrote on the ground.*

[9] *At this, those who heard began to go away one at a time, the older ones first, until only Jesus was left, with the woman still standing*

*there.* [10] *Jesus straightened up and asked her, "Woman, where are they? Has no one condemned you?"*

[11] *"No one, sir," she said.*

*"Then neither do I condemn you," Jesus declared. "Go now and leave your life of sin."*

*— John 8:1-11*

This is how we need to judge others, and I believe that there will be no judgment afterward. Every day ask yourself these questions:

- Have I judged someone based on rumors and lies?
- Have I judged someone based on past?
- Have I judged someone for doing something different?

When you answer these questions, and if you did some of the above, recall how they felt and locate those faults in yourself. Once you are in their shoes, realize how painful it is to undergo judgmental remarks. When we try to find faults in others, it seems to be a fascinating job. But it is no fun at all when you have to go through such sufferings.

We ruin others' lives for what they do or not do, but we forget about what we do when we are behind closed doors; we say and do the same things for which we criticize others. We think that no one is listening to us and forget that God is omnipresent. He is always listening and watching and will show it all on the judgment day.

> [11] *Brothers and sisters, do not slander one another. Anyone who speaks against a brother*

*or sister or judges them speaks against the law and judges it. When you judge the law, you are not keeping it, but sitting in judgment on it.* [12] *There is only one Lawgiver and Judge, the one who is able to save and destroy. But you—who are you to judge your neighbor?*

*— James 4:11-12*

When you bury others in the mud of dishonor, you also get that same mud on yourself. We find it easy to be critical, but we do not try to be self-corrective. Booker T. Washington said, "You can't hold a man down without staying down with him." Criticism expresses that one has a lack of control. Thus, we need to learn to be God-controlled instead of being self-controlled. So, when you tell one how to live or behave, ensure you are right in all you do. For example, you cannot rebuke others for smoking while you puff away in their faces.

Spotting your neighbors' sins is the simplest job, but you need to see your own sins first. Thus, make it your objective to focus on your character and make endeavors to make the best version of yourself.

OK, you have done everything in your power and become the best person on the earth, have you got the rights to judge others?

Well, no, you have not! You cannot judge others because you are righteous. This is not what Jesus has taught to us. He taught us to help and guide others with affection and compassion instead of judging them.

This issue of being judgmental begets another problem, and that is backbiting. Yes, it is another evil in our society. There are people who say that they judge others in their absence and feel Ok with it. Even if you don't judge someone in his/her face, you are still doing the same act. Thus, you have no license, in any way, to judge others in their presence or absence. I plead with you that you do not judge others and stop others if they start such a conversation with you.

> [1] *You, therefore, have no excuse, you who pass judgment on someone else, for at whatever point you judge another, you are condemning yourself, because you who pass judgment do the same things.* [2] *Now we know that God's judgment against those who do such things is based on truth.* [3] *So when you, a mere human being, pass judgment on them and yet do the same things, do you think you will escape God's judgment?*
>
> *— Romans 2:1-3*

# Chapter 8: Be Careful with Your Tongue

*[7] All kinds of animals, birds, reptiles and sea creatures are being tamed and have been tamed by mankind,*

*[8] but no human being can tame the tongue. It is a restless evil, full of deadly poison.*

*[9] With the tongue we praise our Lord and Father, and with it we curse human beings, who have been made in God's likeness.*

*— James 3:7-9*

The tongue is a very sensitive part of our body, and it does wonders, but it is too perilous since it can build up as well as cause devastation. If tongues had locks, many of us could have been better persons.

*[11] Come, my children, listen to me; I will teach you the fear of the Lord. [12] Whoever of you loves life and desires to see many good days, [13] keep your tongue from evil and your lips from telling lies.*

*— Psalm 34:11-13*

As we read this verse, it shows that it is our tongue that triggers the fear of God in our hearts. It is the use of our tongue that makes us good or bad. It is obvious that misuse of the tongue will cause us trouble, and good use will bear sweet fruits.

*Those who guard their lips preserve their lives, but those who speak rashly will come to ruin.*

*— Proverbs 13:3*

The words have their own power, and they represent our personalities. We must realize that the words we speak impact others as well as ourselves. Satan misguided Adam and Eve by using his treacherous and misleading words and brought destruction to them. Our words contain our emotions, feelings, and objectives. Our tongue can cloth our words with anger, envy, etc. Our life manifests what we have said about ourselves and about others. Our tongue controls the happenings in our lives and our destinies. Thus, we must take advantage of the power that God has bestowed us in the form of the tongue. We cannot allow our tongue to go free because it will act like a monster, ready to devour its preys.

We need to take some time and evaluate what we are going to speak, or else we will utter some bad things. Make it a habit to evaluate whatever you speak every day to identify your flaws and take them out of your future conversations with others. Remember that our words do not die but cause serious and lasting troubles. A sword can cause severe injuries and even death. However, the injuries by a sword are healed in some due time. When we injure someone with our words, the healing process takes years, and sometimes the wounds by our words are never healed. A swing of the sword can take life in an instant, but our words can keep killing others for the rest of their lives.

The human tongue seems to be on a rampage and is causing huge destruction across the globe. It is an irony that many people are no more on speaking terms with others because of the tongue as they said bad things. Statesmen deliver deceiving speeches to fool their listeners. In some cases, even clerics do not hesitate to tell a lie when they seek benefit for themselves. There is a famous axiom "As you sow, so shall you reap." It states exactly what we will get if we say bad words about others. Our tongue creates a vicious circle that keeps growing and multiplying.

> *[33] Make a tree good and its fruit will be good, or make a tree bad and its fruit will be bad, for a tree is recognized by its fruit. [34] You brood of vipers, how can you who are evil say anything good? For the mouth speaks what the heart is full of. [35] A good man brings good things out of the good stored up in him, and an evil man brings evil things out of the evil stored up in him. [36] But I tell you that everyone will have to give account on the day of judgment for every empty word they have spoken. [37] For by your*

*words you will be acquitted, and by your words you will be condemned.*

*— Matthew 12:33-37*

The troubles of the tongue are rampant in many societies and affect our lives every day. Sadly, curses are commonplace, and people deliver them as if they were not bad words. A curse goes to the root. Once Jesus cursed a fig tree, and it dried up. The curse goes down to the root, so we should never take it as a trivial matter.

*12 The next day as they were leaving Bethany, Jesus was hungry. 13 Seeing in the distance a fig tree in leaf, he went to find out if it had any fruit. When he reached it, he found nothing but leaves, because it was not the season for figs.*

*14 Then he said to the tree, "May no one ever eat fruit from you again." And his disciples heard him say it.*

*— Mark 11:12-14*

*20 In the morning, as they went along, they saw the fig tree withered from the roots. 21 Peter remembered and said to Jesus, "Rabbi, look! The fig tree you cursed has withered!"*

*22 "Have faith in God," Jesus answered.*

*23 "Truly I tell you, if anyone says to this mountain, 'Go, throw yourself into the sea,' and does not doubt in their heart but believes that what they say will happen, it will be done for them.*

*— Mark 11:20-23*

God forbid, if you happen to be involved in a fight, avoid cursing your opponents, and the same advice I give to couples.

Our tongue becomes extremely poisonous when we are angry as they are produced by our evil nature and wreak havoc. When you are in a state of anger, the best thing to do is to leave that place or stay quiet.

You may have one or two people in your surroundings who let their tongues run as much as they can. They are in the habit of talking so badly that they speak ill things about others, and sometimes they do not even realize it. This is why we should avoid talking unnecessarily. In small talks, we say things that we should not, but it is too late to take your words back, and the troubles arise.

Every word we speak has either a positive or negative effect about whom we talk and cause happiness or sorrow to others. Nobody is perfect in this world, so we have to be even more careful with our tongue because we are responsible for our words. We are all imperfect, and we sin at some point in our life, so we speak ill of others. Remember the story of the woman brought to Jesus who committed adultery and how Jesus made everyone realize of their own sins. To control our tongue, we need to follow the rule of sweeping in front of our own door first.

Though God created human beings in His own image, we do not know the shape of God's body. He gave us His own characteristics, which we can recognize very easily. God asks us to promote love, hope, optimism, compassion, mercy, patience, self-control, and faithfulness. But our tongue hinders our way to reflect such characteristics of our Father God. We get easily angry words if we are taken advantage of and we get upset if things do not go in our favor. Aa a result, we speak negative words about people around us. We even get angry with God if our beloved people meet the maker. It is our frustration, and our tongue supports in releasing it on others.

> *There is one whose rash words are like sword thrusts, but the tongue of the wise brings healing, I tell you, on the day of judgment people will give account for every careless word they speak, for by your words you will be justified, and by your words you will be condemned.*
>
> *— Matthew 12:36-37*

# Chapter 9: Bad Things Happen, But……

*[12] Arise, Lord! Lift up your hand, O God.*

*Do not forget the helpless.*

*[13] Why does the wicked man revile God?*

*Why does he say to himself,*

*"He won't call me to account"?*

*[14] But you, God, see the trouble of the afflicted;*

*you consider their grief and take it in hand.*

*The victims commit themselves to you;*

*you are the helper of the fatherless.*

*[15] Break the arm of the wicked man;*

*call the evildoer to account for his*

*wickedness*

*that would not otherwise be found out.*

*[16] The Lord is King forever and ever;*

*the nations will perish from his land.*

*[17] You, Lord, hear the desire of the afflicted;*

*you encourage them, and you listen to their cry,*

*[18] defending the fatherless and the oppressed,*

*so that mere earthly mortals*

*will never again strike terror.*

*— Psalm 10:12-18*

We often hear the news of flood, famine, earthquake, storms, drought, volcano eruptions, etc. As a result of these natural calamities, tens and thousands of people die. Sometimes, there are little or no warning signs. People in those calamity-struck areas are helpless and suffer from those disasters.

There are many more disasters that take place in people's lives. Parents lose their kids to death, and vice versa; people die of protracted, painful illnesses; people lose their jobs and businesses go down; people misbehave with others and judge them on their race, creed, and past. All these bad things happen in our very world. Wars occur, street crimes occur, and there are lots of other bad things happening around us.

When we see so many bad things happening around us, the negative thoughts arise, and many of us wonder that life is not fair and just, especially when we are helpless. Many people raise this question "what is good in these disasters and why God lets these bad things happen to us. This is when our faith is put to the test. These bad things happen, but there are so many good things happening around the world. If we measure, the good things will certainly outweigh the bad happenings. Thus, God tests us to see who truly believes in Him and sticks to faith in the times of crisis. It is the same Lord who parted the Red Sea, and Israel crossed it with ease, and the same Lord drowned the Egyptian army at the same spot. Thus, none of us has even a single reason to doubt and question God's powers and plans because He is the absolute authority and His plans are the best plans for us. He is the only one Who sends us blessings and He makes us go through trials. In fact, we fail to understand His ways.

We need to submit our will to God, and He will return it with rewards beyond our imagination. When Israelites, under the prophethood of Moses, submitted their will to God, He parted the Red sea for them, and they crossed it with no trouble and no fear. But the Egyptian Pharaoh refused to submit his will to God and he chose to remain arrogant. He was drowned with his army in the same Red Sea. None of us can afford to refuse God's words. Thus, the way to obtain peace and salvation come through our submission to God.

> [1] *God is our refuge and strength, a very present help in trouble.*
>
> [2] *Therefore will not we fear, though the earth be removed, and though the mountains be carried into the midst of the sea;*
>
> [3] *Though the waters thereof roar and be troubled, though the mountains shake with the swelling thereof.*
>
> *— Psalm 46:1-3*

It is alright to have a good bank account, a good job or flourishing business, loving family members, friends, and other relationships. But none of them is a guarantee of happiness and protection against adversaries. The real refuge is with God and God only. We cannot depend on any of our possessions and relations. Our money is not our actual strength but time that we invest in being closer to God. Our appearance and health do not give us help in times of crisis, but God does so, and only He can save us from every bad thing. Deuteronomy 33:27 says, *"The eternal God is your refuge, and underneath are the everlasting arms. He will drive out your enemies before you, saying, 'Destroy them!'*

At times, it seems that everything is against us, and we are destined to be hurt. But we need to understand that every bad thing comes to us as a test. When you believe in this reality, you believe in God's plan, and you become content with whatever is happening in your life. Sometimes, the opposite things happen, and we still seem to be favored by the events that appear to be adverse. Tragedies are a part of life. So are pleasures! Oftentimes, God's wisdom and plans are above and beyond our understanding, but they are always right. In this world, bad things happen to good people too, and this is a hardcore reality of life. This is how nature works, and they never change or are suspended for anyone.

So, we may not have control over what happens to us, but we can manage things afterward. We can prepare ourselves to respond to whatever happens. In fact, we need to make bad things as a source of motivation and repent more and more. We never know how good we are in the eyes of our Lord. Adversaries are not always punishments but a test, and we must pass this test, no matter how tough it is. Just like we remember God in our good times, we should remember God in our bad times. He is the only source who can save us from calamities. We believe that He is our refuge and strength. Psalm 91:1-3 reads. "Surely He shall deliver you from the snare of the fowler and from the perilous pestilence." It is the practice of the righteous people that they always turn to Him in good and bad times.

It is typical human nature to go panicky in adverse situations, but our Lord is comforting. Catastrophic events are real in this world, but God's word is also real, and He promises to help the righteous ones. Thus, we don't need to be afraid of bad things because they neither sustain against God nor against good people. We need to believe that every catastrophe occurs to strengthen us and helps us prepare for the future.

*I have told you these things, so that in me you may have peace. In this world you will have trouble. But take heart! I have overcome the world.*

*— John 16:33*

When we are grieved, we talk to God about the solutions, and He will give us comfort. As we praise Him, we can lament before Him too. He listens to our complaints, and He can respond to them. We cannot harbor ill feelings for God because He knows what is in our hearts. Thus, we need to let go what is killing and rotting inside our minds. In adverse situations, God is the one Who can lodge your complaints, so cry it out before God. Be insistent just like kids do before us. And why I say like a child! Of course, we are His children, and we can insist on asking for assistance before our Father. A prayer of lament is a tool we can use to ease our sufferings and deliver us from pain. So, use this powerful tool to overcome all adversaries in your life.

# Chapter 10: Inner Peace: Your Source of Solace

*But he was pierced for our transgressions,*

*he was crushed for our iniquities;*

*the punishment that brought us peace was on him,*

*and by his wounds we are healed.*

*— Isaiah 53:5*

When they captured Jesus with the intention to crucify, Jesus delivered a great message to his disciples, and it is something we all desire to have in our troubled world today.

*Peace I leave with you; my peace I give you. I do not give to you as the world gives. Do not let your hearts be troubled and do not be afraid.*
*— John 14:27*

God brought us with the body and blood of Jesus. He sacrificed his life for our sins, and we received the peace of Jesus. Yet, we are troubled today. We have given room to so many fears in our lives; we are concerned about our protection, health, finances, future, kids, and their future and many more concerns. We are surrounded by too many worries. We start off our days with a sulky mood. We have lost our tolerance level, so even a petty issue at time ruins our whole day. We toil every day to find peace and solace among the worries of life, but it seems that we have been robbed of peace. In such a turbulent life, finding inner peace is like looking for a needle in a haystack, but it is very much possible.

> *Let the peace of Christ rule in your hearts, since as members of one body you were called to peace. And be thankful.*
>
> *— Colossians 3:15*

As I go through a few pieces of news, I find nothing but absolute chaos in this world. Neighbors fight neighbors; office colleagues envy progressive colleagues; countries fight other countries; cold wars are going on and what not! In such a raging world, how can we even think of finding inner peace? Jesus made a great sacrifice, but we have ruined or lost it with our hands. We are in search of inner peace, and we are trying to find it in the outer world. "Inner peace" is a self-defining term. Thus, we need to look inside our souls, and we will see that inner peace waiting to be found by us. Of course, there are troubles everywhere, and peace and troubles are opposite to each other. Until we are troubled, we cannot see inner peace.

Jesus taught so many things to find inner peace, and he ultimately laid his life down so that we could be at peace. Jesus said that he gave us his peace. Today, we are at fault that we cannot see it, find it, and include it in our lives. Peace is hidden in our plain sight, but we have turned a blind eye to it. In fact, we do not bother to even look at peace. Jesus said that there would always be wars or rumors of war (Matthew 24:6). Because of our sins, finding inner peace appears to be a dream until Jesus Christ returns. However, it is never too late to make an effort, and this is what God wants us to do, i.e., find peace through the way He told us.

> *He will wipe every tear from their eyes. There will be no more death' or mourning or crying or pain, for the old order of things has passed away.*
>
> *— Revelation 21:4*

The peace that Jesus gave to his disciples is actually for us too. Yes, his peace if for us too, and it is a complete package of peace, so it will bring an absolute state of tranquility in our lives. Do you know the beauty of Christian faith? We get purer and better and find peace as we go through hardships. Does it sound superficial? Well, it may, but it is 100% true and practical. Our mind is an amazing gift of God, and it can do wonders when it comes to finding inner peace. So, the best thing we can do is learn how to control our mind and get rid of negative feelings. If our mind is focused on God and good things, we can achieve inner peace.

We experience different feelings, and anger is one of the most difficult feelings to manage. Anger is an arch-enemy of inner peace, so both cannot live together. If you are a calm and composed person, or you have some in your circle, remember when or someone else was in the state of anger! The whole new person emerges, and that person is not likable. Jesus is peace, and we have to live through Jesus to get a peaceful life.

Envy and jealousy are also the worst enemies of inner peace. They deprive you of good moments of celebration. For example, if your colleague has been promoted, and he holds a party to celebrate, you go and enjoy the celebratory moments there. If you sulk sitting at home, it will not do any good to you either. That opportunity is gone. Accept this fact and prepare to grab the next opportunity, but be fair and avoid playing foul games. Being jealous of your colleagues will harbor ill feelings in your heart and kick the peace out of it. A heart full of bad feelings cannot be a welcoming place for Jesus and God.

The human mind is very tricky and can fool you to believe that you have a good heart. Thus, you give control of your mind to the Lord, and there will be no doubt that you have a pure heart, filled with inner peace. Doing so is a tough job because sufferings and greed can derail us easily, but the believers do it anyway. Persistence in your thoughts and effort is the key to success here. We are short-sighted and lose interest easily, but it is a matter of life, good and peaceful life. It is difficult, but the rewards are much greater.

> *Cast all your anxiety on him because he cares for you.*
>
> *— 1 Peter 5:7*

# Chapter 11: The Power of Humility

*[1] Therefore if you have any encouragement from being united with Christ, if any comfort from his love, if any common sharing in the Spirit, if any tenderness and compassion,*

*[2] then make my joy complete by being like-minded, having the same love, being one in spirit and of one mind.*

*[3] Do nothing out of selfish ambition or vain conceit. Rather, in humility value others above yourselves,*

*[4] not looking to your own interests but each of you to the interests of the others.*

*[5] In your relationships with one another, have the same mindset as Christ Jesus:*

*[6] Who, being in very nature God, did not consider equality with God something to be used to his own advantage;*

*[7] rather, he made himself nothing by taking the very nature of a servant, being made in human likeness.*

*[8] And being found in appearance as a man, he humbled himself by becoming obedient to death—even death on a cross!*

*— Philippians 2:1-9*

After God, who could be the highest, the best in this universe?

Of course, Jesus.

The above verses are a plea from Paul to the Philippians. These verses show us the exact picture of humility. The life of Jesus is an epitome of humility, and we need no more reason to behave with humility when it was a way of Jesus. We can't be more thankful to Jesus for showing us how we should live since it leads us to the peak of humanity. Humility means to have the quality of having a modest or low view of one's importance. Though it means to keep yourself low, it actually takes you to the peak. In the eyes of God, the lowest in nature is at the highest point. The humble ones win the favor of God, and it is the biggest achievement for us.

> *In the same way, you who are younger, submit yourselves to your elders. All of you, clothe yourselves with humility toward one another, because God opposes the proud but shows favor to the humble.*
>
> *— 1 Peter 5:5*

In today's world, we have a grave crisis of unity, and one of the basic reasons is a lack of humility among peoples and groups. Arrogance is the opposite of humility; thus, an arrogant person lacks humility. The problem is that we have a never-ending supply in plenty. We simply do not want to follow orders. We want to boss around, and we forget that it contradicts with the teachings of Jesus. We forget that Jesus has the highest status, and humility is one of his traits. We think that we can be independent and rule others, but we forget that we are servants to God Who is kind and ignores many of our follies.

In the USA, 40 to 50% of married couples divorce, but the worst part is that men and women opt to live in sin, that we simply call a live-in relationship or a LAT relationship. It may not mean that they do not love each other and do not believe in "until death do us part." But they do not want to be in holy matrimony, so they have no legal responsibility of each other. The problem lies in being egotistic and unwilling to listen to others. When we lack humility, we are arrogant, self-centered, egotistic, and what not. We need to understand the importance of humility and how its absence leads to our problems. It becomes difficult to collaborate when neither of the parties is humble.

> *Are there any of you who are wise and understanding? You are to prove it by your good life, by your good deeds performed with humility and wisdom.*
>
> — James 3:13

Humility trains us to be in low estate and consider others at a higher status. They care for others and are always ready to sacrifice for others. They have no desire to be higher than others and claim the best positions. Matthew 23:12 tells us, "For those who exalt themselves will be humbled, and those who humble themselves will be exalted." This verse is a great source of inspiration to adopt humble ways. All our lives, we remain the children of God and Jesus referred to people as "little children," and it is a perfect description for us. Before God, we are small, and we have to be like that with our fellow beings too.

> [3] *And he said: "Truly I tell you, unless you change and become like little children, you will never enter the kingdom of heaven.* [4] *Therefore,*

*whoever takes the lowly position of this child is the greatest in the kingdom of heaven.*

*— Matthews 18:3-4*

Being humble does not mean that we are inferior or weaker than others, but it is a realistic assessment of our condition. Humility shows us how God sees us. On the contrary, arrogance is actually weak and disgraceful. Humility fills your life with harmony since you can see that God has been merciful to you. God loves us all, but we cannot take it for granted; we have to prove ourselves worthy of God's love and mercy and His sonship. Luke 17:10 describes our condition in perfect words, *"I am an unworthy servant of the Lord; I am only doing what it is my duty to do."* I advise that you do not make your shortcomings an excuse of not being humble. I have seen people grieving about their frustrations and negative behaviors, but they are merely lame excuses. Humility is not bound to any of your personal and physical states.

Another important point is that humility is not about showing off yourself. If you are humble to God's love, you do not need to declare it. Just like arrogance, humility shows up itself. It is a practice that you do every day, all through your life. I assure you that humility is a source that will take you to the extreme heights of success and spirituality.

# Chapter 12: God is Right in Front of You the Whole Time.

*35 For I was hungry and you gave me something to eat, I was thirsty and you gave me something to drink, I was a stranger and you invited me in,*

*36 I needed clothes and you clothed me, I was sick and you looked after me, I was in prison and you came to visit me.'*

*37 "Then the righteous will answer him, 'Lord, when did we see you hungry and feed you, or thirsty and give you something to drink?*

*38 When did we see you a stranger and invite you in, or needing clothes and clothe you?*

*39 When did we see you sick or in prison and go to visit you?'*

*40 "The King will reply, 'Truly I tell you, whatever you did for one of the least of these brothers and sisters of mine, you did for me.'*
*— Matthew 25:35-40*

Excuse me! Are you looking for Jesus, God, the Holy Spirit?

It is simple. Jesus, God, the Holy Spirit are in the bible, right? Recite the verses, and you have found them!

I wish finding God could be that easy! Reciting the bible verses is just the beginning of finding these holy entities.

Bible is our guide to find God, but we have to find Him in our surroundings, and the first thing to do is find and follow Jesus.

*I am the way, and the truth, and the life; no one comes to the Father but through Me.*

*— John 14:6*

*Then Jesus again spoke to them, saying, "I am the Light of the world; he who follows Me will not walk in the darkness, but will have the Light of life."*

*— John 8:12*

The simplest way to find God is to look into your heart and soul because God dwells in our hearts. Thus, we must know and embrace other people, i.e., our family, friends, and even strangers. We are the key sources to find God as we show love and sympathy to others.

Let me tell you an even simpler formula to see God. We know that God is positive energy, and Satan is negative energy, and neither of them exudes the opposite to their energies. The acts that are negative and spread bad things cannot be from God; they are certainly from Satan. If you start discarding those negative energies from your life, you will keep getting closer to God. Though inch by inch, you can reduce the distance between God and you. These negative energies come from grudge, envy, jealousy, hatred, contempt, arrogance, unrighteous anger, greed, pessimism, and other things in this vein. As soon as you get rid of these ill emotions and acts, you will find your heart filled with God's love.

God is found in every act of kindness, no matter how small it is! If you remove scattered stone on the pathway, you can save others from falling and hurting themselves. It is a small act and just requires a slight kick, but this act is not petty in weight before God. Bad things gang up fast, and we have to ensure that we promote acts of kindness fast, and we will find God even faster.

Jesus emphasizes on helping others in need in all possible ways we can. The verses I quoted *(Matthew 25:35-40)* at the beginning of this chapter reveal us the minute details of finding God. Feeding a hungry person or offering water to a thirsty person is not a big deal, but we can never undermine their importance. These small acts are the means of getting closer to God.

Our children are a gift from God, but they come with responsibility. If we fulfill that responsibility, we follow God's command. Yes, nurturing children with discipline and faith demands hard work. We need great reserves of affection, peace, kindness, self-control, and patience. This way, we bring up good Christians who follow Jesus and spread goodness further.

> *Train up a child in the way he should go; even when he is old, he will not depart from it.*
>
> *— Proverbs 22:6*

> *Discipline your children, and they will give you peace; they will bring you the delights you desire.*
>
> *— Proverbs 29:17*

## Chapter 13: God's Gracious Promises

Every word in the bible is the word of God and has a powerful and life-altering impact. There are many verses in the bible that admonish the wrongdoers and sinners, but with a hope of forgiveness if one repents.

> *Be on your guard! If your brother sins, rebuke him; and if he repents, forgive him.*
>
> *— Luke 17:3*

God is ever-ready to deliver us from our sins and miseries. The Bible is our source for finding solace as we go through the promises of God, and He never goes against His promises. These promises are the source of happiness and satisfaction if we follow the word of God. It does not matter what problem we are facing if we have absolute faith in God. We can get rid of every existing issue in our world, such as addictions, sins, financial problems, depression, a failed marriage, bad health, fear, anxiety, and others.

A promise is a declaration that is held between two people or parties where one promises to do exactly what they say. We also make promises to our friends and family members. Sometimes, we break our promises or remain unsuccessful in keeping our words. It must have happened to you, maybe, more than once. It has happened to me. Sometimes, circumstances do not allow us. We are human beings and depend on God's will. We cannot move even an inch if it is not God's will. How could we ensure to keep our promises when we do not own our lives, our words, our action, and our possessions? Despite all our strength, we are dependent on God's will.

Our Lord is free of dependence, and His promises are carved in stone. When our Lord makes a promise to us, it will indeed come to pass. The Bible is filled with the many great promises of God, and they are no empty promises. They have been sealed by the Highest Authority in this universe, our God, and they have been reassured by Jesus Christ himself and his disciples on a number of occasions.

I feel elated when I go through the holy scripture where God has made us great promises, and I know He will keep all of His promises, no matter what! I want to show you how gracious our God is, and how He is going to reward us for our good deeds and pardon us for our sins. I have assorted many of Gods promises that will help you strengthen your faith in God. These biblical verses about God's promises are meant to encourage you and shape your life accordingly. Read these gracious promises and allow them to enter into the heart, and you will certainly be saved.

> *Let the wicked forsake his way and the unrighteous man his thoughts; and let him return to the LORD, And He will have compassion on him, And to our God, For He will abundantly pardon.*
>
> *— Isaiah 55:7*

> *And because of his glory and excellence, he has given us great and precious promises. These are the promises that enable you to share his divine nature and escape the world's corruption caused by human desires.*
>
> *— 2 Peter 1:4*

*For I know the plans I have for you," says the Lord. "They are plans for good and not for disaster, to give you a future and a hope.*

*— Jeremiah 29:11*

*If we confess our sins, He is faithful and righteous to forgive us our sins and to cleanse us from all unrighteousness.*

*— 1 John 1:9*

*Come to me, all you who are weary and burdened, and I will give you rest. Take my yoke upon you and learn from me, for I am gentle and humble in heart, and you will find rest for your souls.*

*— Matthew 11:28-29*

*I have wiped out your transgressions like a thick cloud and your sins like a heavy mist return to Me, for I have redeemed you.*

*— Isaiah 44:22*

*And this same God who takes care of me will supply all your needs from his glorious riches, which have been given to us in Christ Jesus.*

*— Philippians 4:19*

*For God gave us a spirit not of fear but of power and love and self-control.*

*— 2 Timothy 1:7*

*But all who listen to me will live in peace, untroubled by fear of harm."*

*— Proverbs 1:33*

*I have come as Light into the world, so that everyone who believes in Me will not remain in darkness.*

*— John 12:46*

*Be strong and courageous. Do not be afraid; do not be discouraged, for the LORD your God will be with you wherever you go.*

*— Joshua 1:9*

*"I am leaving you with a gift—peace of mind and heart. And the peace I give is a gift the world cannot give. So, don't be troubled or afraid.*

*— John 14:27*

*Then I will sprinkle clean water on you, and you will be clean; I will cleanse you from all your filthiness and from all your idols.*

*— Ezekiel 36:25*

*If you confess with your mouth that Jesus is Lord and believe in your heart that God raised him from the dead, you will be saved.*

*— Romans 10:9*

*For all the promises of God in Him are Yes, and in Him Amen, to the glory of God through us.*

*— 2 Corinthians 1:20*

*He gives strength to the weary and increases the power of the weak.*

*— Isaiah 40:29*

*but those who hope in the LORD will renew their strength. They will soar on wings like eagles; they will run and not grow weary, they will walk and not be faint.*

*— Isaiah 40:31*

*If any of you lacks wisdom, you should ask God, who gives generously to all without finding fault, and it will be given to you.*

*— James 1:5*

*The LORD himself goes before you and will be with you; he will never leave you nor forsake you. Do not be afraid; do not be discouraged."*

*— Deuteronomy 31:8*

Our Lord is our great strength and motivation to do good deeds, and He will reward us abundantly. We know that He will keep every one of His promises, yet we deviate from His instructed path. My brothers and sisters, I implore you to listen to your heart, and you will actually listen to God's voice. Follow that voice, and you will find that only God's words are true and will save you from every evil and every sin in this world.

# Chapter 14: But I'm too Bad to Be Rewarded & Forgiven!

> *If my people, who are called by my name, will humble themselves and pray and seek my face and turn from their wicked ways, then I will hear from heaven, and I will forgive their sin and will heal their land.*
>
> *— 2 Chronicles 7:14*

*"I'm too bad. I don't think God will ever forgive me. I'll have to live with my miseries."* There are millions of people who think this way. So, if you also think this way, you are not alone. You may have one or more people angry with you in your life, and they may not forgive you so easily. But asking for forgiveness to God is way too simple, and He is ever-

embracing and ever-forgiving. Jesus Christ never leaves the astray sheep alone.

It is not hard to think that God is ever-willing to forgive us the first time we sin and repent, particularly if we learn from our mistakes and promise to stop committing sins. What about after repentance, when we have promised to stop committing sins of any kind. In fact, the majority of us do not learn from mistakes and keep on doing bad deeds. Is God really gracious enough to forgive us in spite of repeating sins?

It is an important question, and it also kept the Apostle Paul restless when he penned the words of the holy scriptures. To find an accurate answer, we need to understand how God's forgiveness works, our need, ourselves and our nature, and our Savior.

The Apostle Paul struggles with his thoughts and says that he has the opportunity to do good deeds in the eyes of God every day and he is willing to do good deeds because he is thankful to God for God brought him to Jesus. In the state of confusion, he writes:

> [15] *I do not understand what I do. For what I want to do I do not do, but what I hate I do.* [16] *And if I do what I do not want to do, I agree that the law is good.* [17] *As it is, it is no longer I myself who do it, but it is sin living in me.*
>
> — *Romans 7:15-16*

The Apostle Paul admits that he is confronted with situations where he knows exactly what the right thing is to do. But he also gets frightened when he did something different from what he wanted to do. He faces such situations many times in his life.

He finds himself in confusion when he knows the damaging effects that his bad actions will bring on his life, but he does them anyway. It is a situation like a chronic alcoholic who is aware of the fact they one more sip will damage his body organs, but he keeps on drinking. Paul is aware of the fact that every bad action will bring consequences, and he knows that God's law is always right because it keeps him from harms and sufferings. There is a constant battle going in Paul's mind and soul, and he further says to identify the cause of the problem:

> [18] *For I know that good itself does not dwell in me, that is, in my sinful nature. For I have the desire to do what is good, but I cannot carry it out.* [19] *For I do not do the good I want to do, but the evil I do not want to do—this I keep on*

*doing.* [20] *Now if I do what I do not want to do, it is no longer I who do it, but it is sin living in me that does it.*

*— Romans 7:18-20*

We can see that the Apostle Paul's sins cause him the problems, and he is in desperate need of forgiveness, and only God can offer him solace and forgiveness.

Today, our story is no different from the Apostle Paul. Our lives are full of sins, and we need to admit that we get filthy in a sinful life every day. We know it well, and we want to do better, but we pull ourselves back to sin. The Apostle Paul's admittance of recurrently falling for sins and repentance teach us the importance of being in constant contact with God. It reminds us that we can never remain pure if we deviate from the path of God. If we leave God's path, we are at high risk of getting consumed by our so-called self-righteousness and whatever good deeds we may do. No matter what we do, we remain sinners, so we are always in need of the forgiveness that only our Lord can offer to all of us. In fact, we cannot afford to distract ourselves for even a single second from God's words. Yet we live most of our lives without paying attention to God's words.

Do you realize how God keeps forgiving us, even when we don't ask for forgiveness? He is indeed forgiving!

As we try to understand God's way of forgiveness, first, we need to understand our sinfulness. When searching for God's forgiveness, we need to realize that there is nothing we have done, and we cannot do anything worthwhile to get God's forgiveness.

The Apostle Paul tells us clearly that we live with two natures, both saint and evil at the same time. We are saints as God has brought us to faith and created a new spirit within us, which Paul refers to as inner being and it delights in God's law.

As for the evil, Paul says that it is also the nature we are born with, and it is hostile to God. Thus, this negative side of our nature is always up to corrupting good things. Similarly, the inner being also hates evil. However, evil reveals itself in thoughts and actions. In our minds and soul, both the natures keep on conflicting with each other. Neither of them is willing to give up. This battle goes on until one of them gains absolute control over the other. So, this fight continues all our lives. Now when you think that you are too bad to be forgiven, it is the evil inside, trying to make you give up on good deeds so that you can live in sin forever.

As soon as you stop feeling the burden of sins on your mind and soul, it indicates that your inner being, your good soul is dead. If you are not bothered by a sinful act, your evil nature has won out. This battle goes on until it indicates that your good nature is struggling against your sinful nature. It also indicates that you are not away from God's forgiveness. If you repent, you will be forgiven because your soul is not dead yet. You just need to find your true Savior and ask for help to defeat your evil nature.

Paul found Jesus as his savior, and he is our savior too. Jesus offered Paul forgiveness by condemning Paul's sinful nature. Jesus said to Paul on the way to Damascus:

*He fell to the ground and heard a voice say to him, "Saul, Saul, why do you persecute me?"*

*— Acts 9:4*

Christ guided the Apostle Paul to see his sins and he told in the following words:

*What a wretched man I am! Who will rescue me from this body that is subject to death?*

*— Romans 7:24*

Here, you can see how desperate and helpless Paul felt, but he was forgiven because he found and believed in Jesus Christ.

When he was healed from his sins, he further wrote in Romans in different chapters:

*[22] This righteousness is given through faith in Jesus Christ to all who believe. There is no difference between Jew and Gentile, [23] for all have sinned and fall short of the glory of God, [24] and all are justified freely by his grace through the redemption that came by Christ Jesus.*

*— Romans 3:22-24*

*Thanks be to God, who delivers me through Jesus Christ our Lord!*

*So then, I myself in my mind am a slave to God's law, but in my sinful nature a slave to the law of sin.*

*— Romans 7:25*

Satan is our enemy, and he never wants us to be forgiven. Thus, our evil nature presents us with a list of our sins and persuades us to lose hope for forgiveness. The evil makes us believe that Jesus will not forgive us for our sins. The people who are trapped by this trick, they get on a spree to grow the number of their sins and do not hesitate to fulfill their bad desires. The next time you have this thought of being unforgiven, be happy because your good inner being is very much alive and fighting against the evil.

## Chapter 15: The sands are running out!

As soon as we come into this world, one undeniable truth is death, the end of life. No matter how rich, influential, strong, or healthy we are, no one on earth can escape death. According to the latest statistics, the average life expectancy for Americans is 78.7 years. In the UK, Canada, and Australia, the figures of average life expectancy are marginally higher. Though no one can tell the exact age of Jesus Christ when he was crucified, it is guessed to be between 33 and 36. As compared to our age, it is a fairly young age when Jesus met the maker.

In such a short span of life, Jesus Christ taught us everything delivered to him by God. His teachings are eternal and lay the foundation for our righteous lives. Living a long life was never a desire of Jesus but submitting his will to God. Even when he was on the cross, he agreed with the will of God. Jesus knew that God's will was always better than his will. Thus, he lived a life bound to God's will, and he never complained. He taught us to live our lives according to God's will because that is the only right way of living.

The governments run a Witness Protection Program or a Witness Security Program. This program is designed to protect threatened witnesses before, during, and after a trial. Once a person or family is involved in this program, it is the responsibility of the government to protect those people and help them live a normal life. The government does so if the witness(es) follow the rules and regulation told by the government. In the same way, we live our lives under the protection program run by God. We are constantly listened to and watched by God, and He keeps His promises in every condition.

> *The Lord will keep you from all harm; He will watch over your life; the Lord will watch over your coming and going, both now and forevermore.*
>
> *— Psalm 121:7-8*

Remember the sands are running out. The clock of life is constantly ticking. We have to perform our responsibilities right in this life and make our way in the good book of God and Christ. God will give us many chances to mend our ways, but there will be no second chance once the death clutches our souls. Instead of giving our wretched souls to death, let's start following the ways of Jesus and depart from this world with a happy soul. In the previous chapter, you read plenty of God's gracious promises, and He will keep each and every of the promise provided that we do not lack in performing our duties.

In the next chapter, I will tell you some very powerful prayers that will help you find true success and peace of life and will help you embrace God and His teachings.

## Chapter 16: Prayers in the Bible

Prayer is one superpower that can stand alone to win against all the odds. No matter how many, how severe, and what kind of adversaries you are facing, pray to seek forgiveness and mercy with pure heart, and your prayers will certainly be answered. It is only God who we need to look up to, always. And never hesitate whatever you want to ask in your prayers. He is the Lord of this universe, and He possesses absolute power over everything and every living being present in this universe. Our Lord is not a boss in an office who has limitations to fulfill our requests, whereas a majority of them has no big heart to entertain even small requests. Here, we are talking about the sole master of this universe who has already shown us a number of miracles.

So, why hesitate when praying to God? I always say that you go big, as big as you can and want when you pray. Ask for His blessings and mercy in abundance. It is only WE who have limitations, but He does not! And always pray with conviction.

> *Therefore, I tell you, whatever you ask for in prayer, believe that you have received it, and it will be yours.*
>
> *— Mark 11:24*

> *This is the confidence we have in approaching God: that if we ask anything according to his will, he hears us.*
>
> *— 1 John 5:14*

Thus, you need to firmly believe in your prayers, and our Lord is gracious, merciful, and powerful to accept our prayers and reward us with great treasures. Prayer may seem a monologue, where you utter a few words in a normal or loud voice or in your heart, but it is never ever a monologue!

Prayer is always a dialogue! It is a dialogue between you and the Lord. The next time you pray, believe in this fact that you are talking to God and He is listening attentively. In your praying dialogue, He is the Listener and the Answerer. I love this analogical quote by Arthur Hopkins that makes it clear how our prayers work.

> *Our prayer and God's mercy are like two buckets in a well; while one ascends, the other descends.*

*— Arthur Hopkins*

Interestingly, this is not my suggestion or anyone else's suggestion that we all should pray. This suggestion comes directly from our Lord. He is the most merciful, and He asks us to pray and repent when we do not obey His commands and commit sins through various acts.

*Then you will call on me and come and pray to me, and I will listen to you.*

*— Jeremiah 29:12*

*If we confess our sins, he is faithful and just and will forgive us our sins and purify us from all unrighteousness.*

*— 1 John 1:9*

*Do not be anxious about anything, but in everything, by prayer and petition, with thanksgiving, present your requests to God.*
*— Philippians 4:6*

*Call to me and I will answer you and tell you great and unsearchable things you do not know.*
*— Jeremiah 33:3*

When you pray to God, do not restrict your prayers to yourself only. Do not be a miser in your prayers, but you be generous and pray for others too! This is the beauty of prayers that God rewards us for our prayers and to those as well for whom we pray. I believe that our prayers for others are powerful tools that will help us create universal harmony.

*Therefore, confess your sins to each other and pray for each other so that you may be healed. The prayer of a righteous man is powerful and effective.*

*— James 5:16*

*But to you who are listening I say: Love your enemies, do good to those who hate you, bless those who curse you, pray for those who mistreat you.*

*— Luke 6:27-28*

Praying is a practice that every prophet needed, and even Jesus Christ himself turned to prayers when he needed to have spiritual refreshment. In our words, when Christ needed a break and to recharge his batteries, he turned to prayers, often in solitude. It was also a time when he needed to spend some time with God. Elijah, Issacs, Jacob, Moses, Isaiah, Amos Hosea, Jeremiah, and Abraham, they always prayed to God when they needed help, strength, and they thanked God through prayers to keep them on the righteous path.

> *But Jesus Himself would often slip away to the wilderness and pray.*
>
> *— Luke 5:16*

> *After He had sent the crowds away, He went up on the mountain by Himself to pray; and when it was evening, He was there alone.*
>
> *— Matthew 14:23*

*In the early morning, while it was still dark, Jesus got up, left the house, and went away to a secluded place, and was praying there.*

*—Mark 1:35*

*It was at this time that He went off to the mountain to pray, and He spent the whole night in prayer to God.*

*— Luke 6:12*

The apostles were fortunate enough to get the teachings by Jesus Christ directly, and they, too, followed and lived up to what Jesus Christ taught them. We should also be thankful to the apostles and other resources who transmitted the teachings of Jesus to us.

As the Apostles observed Jesus closely, they noticed that their prayers were not as powerful as Jesus Christ had. Thus, they became curious to learn better ways of praying.

Today, we think that we can utter a few words, and they will be good enough to qualify as "prayers." Of course, God loves us and always listens to our prayers, though how empty and clumsy our words maybe! Nevertheless, it is best that we learn the ways how Jesus and his apostles prayed to God, and this is the best way to seek salvation.

The apostles knew often repeated prayers of the Torah. They noted that Jesus prayed with a sort of authority and power which they had never seen before. Jesus prayed as if he were talking to God, and God was listening to Jesus. And this is why I say that your prayer is a dialogue.

So, the apostles approached Jesus and asked Jesus to teach them the ways to pray instead of asking for more prayers. And they got the following answer which is a guiding principle for all of us too:

> *[5] And when you pray, do not be like the hypocrites, for they love to pray standing in the synagogues and on the street corners to be seen by others. Truly I tell you, they have received their reward in full. [6] But when you pray, go into your room, close the door and pray to your Father, who is unseen. Then your Father, who sees what is done in secret, will reward you. [7] And when you pray, do not keep on babbling like pagans, for they think they will be heard because of their many words. [8] Do not be like*

*them, for your Father knows what you need*

*before you ask him.*

*[9] This, then, is how you should pray:*

*Our Father in heaven,*

*hallowed be your name,*

*[10] your kingdom come,*

*your will be done,*

*on earth as it is in heaven.*

*[11] Give us today our daily bread.*

*[12] And forgive us our debts,*

*as we also have forgiven our debtors.*

*[13] And lead us not into temptation,*

*but deliver us from the evil one.*

*— Matthew 6:5-13*

As you can see, pray is a powerful weapon, and it works best when we follow all the protocols to use it. Here I share a few tips to make your prayers more powerful.

As I said earlier, prayer is a dialogue with God, so we need to start this dialogue by addressing to whom we are speaking by name, and this is our Lord. Jesus Christ starts prayers by saying, "Our Father in heaven." Thus, Jesus showed us how to start our prayers. When you pray, start by saying, "Our Father in heaven" or "Father God."

There is nothing better than thanking God when praying? An honest "thank you" is a good starter for prayers. Imagine how happy our parents are when we thank them for providing us with many things in our lives. How happy he would be when we thank the One who has given us life. God has already too many great things for us. He heals us when we are sick, and He gives us the strength to surmount difficulties. He is the only one who can answer our prayers; thus, He deserves praise and praise opens the gates of heaven.

God owns every single inch in this universe, and He is too gracious that He has given it to us. But everything happens with His will and command. Thus, we need to submit our will to our Lord. And this is what Jesus taught at the time of the crucifixion.

Crucifixion was the most difficult time for Jesus. He had to face one of the most agonizing and disgraceful punishments, death on a cross. Jesus took on sin and death for us:

> *For God made Christ, who never sinned, to be the offering for our sin, so that we could be made right with God through Christ.*
>
> *— 2 Corinthians 5:21*

When he was taken to a dark and isolated hillside in the Garden of Gethsemane, he knew what was waiting for him. As a man, he did not want to suffer the physical torture of death by crucifixion. As the Son of God, he could not understand the awaiting separation. But He never lost his faith in God and prayed with absolute submission.

> *Father, if you are willing, take this cup from me; yet not my will, but yours be done.*
>
> *— Luke 22:42*

> *He went on a little farther and bowed with his face to the ground, praying, "My Father! If it is possible, let this cup of suffering be taken away from me. Yet I want your will to be done, not mine.*
>
> *— Matthew 26:39*

Jesus was in agony as his sweat trickled with blood on the cross.

> *And being in anguish, he prayed more earnestly, and his sweat was like drops of blood falling to the ground.*
>
> *— Luke 22:44*

In spite of being in severe agony, Jesus did not ask for taking the pain away, but he surrendered to God’s will as he said, "Not my will, but yours be done." Jesus lived his life that way. He always submitted his will to God and obeyed every command.

> *For I have come down from heaven not to do my will but to do the will of him who sent me."*
>
> *— John 6:38*

I know it is a very difficult task to let our wants and desires go away over God's will. But Jesus did it, even at the time of suffering. Obedience and submission to God are the key ingredients to make our prayers more powerful. Jesus called us to follow him and learn obedience through suffering as he did:

> *Even though Jesus was God's Son, he learned obedience from the things he suffered. In this way, God qualified him as a perfect High Priest, and he became the source of eternal salvation for all those who obey him.*
>
> *— Hebrews 5:8-9*

God knows how weak we are and He will not test us more than we can endure. We just need to let go our stubborn will and submit to God. When we have absolute faith in our Lord, we will gain the strength to let go of our desires. Let me assure you that His will is perfect for us and will do the best things for us. God has great plans for those who love Him.

If and when you are not sure what you should pray, thankfully, the bible is always here to guide us with eternal gems of prayers for all situations. There is myriad of prayers in the bible for a multitude of occasions. I have assorted some very powerful and comprehensive biblical prayers so that we all can ask for great and fulfilling lives.

> *Answer me when I call to you, my righteous God. Give me relief from my distress; have mercy on me and hear my prayer.*
>
> *— Psalm 4:1*

*If it is true that you look favorably on me, let me know your ways so I may understand you more fully and continue to enjoy your favor.*

*— Exodus 33:13*

*Blessed be the God and Father of our Lord Jesus Christ! According to his great mercy, he has caused us to be born again to a living hope through the resurrection of Jesus Christ from the dead.*

*— 1 Peter 1:3*

*Oh, that You would bless me and expand my territory! Please be with me in all that I do, and keep me from all trouble and pain!*

*— 1 Chronicles 4:10*

*God, I've heard what our ancestors say about You, and I'm stopped in my tracks, down on my knees. Do among us what You did among them. Work among us as you worked among them.*

*— Habakkuk 3:2, The Message*

[29] *Give us, your servants, great boldness in preaching Your word.*

[30] *Stretch out Your hand with healing power; may miraculous signs and wonders be done through the name of Your holy servant Jesus.*

*— Acts 4:29-30*

[1] *Have mercy on me, O God, according to your steadfast love; according to your abundant mercy blot out my transgressions.*

[2] *Wash me thoroughly from my iniquity, and cleanse me from my sin!*

*— Psalm 51:1-2*

[7] *Cleanse me with hyssop, and I will be clean;*

*wash me, and I will be whiter than snow.*

[8] *Let me hear joy and gladness;*

*let the bones you have crushed rejoice.*

[9] *Hide your face from my sins*

*and blot out all my iniquity.*

[10] *Create in me a pure heart, O God,*

*and renew a steadfast spirit within me.*

[11] *Do not cast me from your presence*

*or take your Holy Spirit from me.*

[12] *Restore to me the joy of your salvation*

*and grant me a willing spirit, to sustain me.*

*— Psalm 51:7-12*

*[1] Have mercy on me, O God,*

*according to your steadfast love;*

*according to your abundant mercy*

*blot out my transgressions.*

*[2] Wash me thoroughly from my iniquity,*

*and cleanse me from my sin.*

*— Psalm 51*

*[9] God, whom I serve in my spirit in preaching the gospel of his Son, is my witness how constantly I remember you*

*[10] in my prayers at all times; and I pray that now at last by God's will the way may be opened for me to come to you.*

*— Romans 1:9-10*

*[14] For this reason I kneel before the Father,*

*[15] from whom every family in heaven and on earth derives its name.*

*[16] I pray that out of his glorious riches he may strengthen you with power through his Spirit in your inner being,*

*[17] so that Christ may dwell in your hearts through faith. And I pray that you, being rooted and established in love,*

*[18] may have power, together with all the Lord's holy people, to grasp how wide and long and high and deep is the love of Christ,*

*[19] and to know this love that surpasses knowledge—that you may be filled to the measure of all the fullness of God.*

*— Ephesians 3:14-19*

It is best that you memorize these prayers and also help your children to memorize them. I know children will be much faster at memorizing them. In fact, it is a lifetime gift you can give to your children and to yourself.

All Glory be to God!!

Made in the USA
Monee, IL
17 March 2022